30 Days in The Word

DAILY DEVOTIONAL

BY SHARNA KNOWLES

Suite 300 - 990 Fort St
Victoria, BC, V8V 3K2
Canada

www.friesenpress.com

Copyright © 2021 by Sharna Knowles
First Edition — 2021

All rights reserved.

No part of this publication may be reproduced in any form, or by any means, electronic or mechanical, including photocopying, recording, or any information browsing, storage, or retrieval system, without permission in writing from FriesenPress.

ISBN
978-1-5255-9383-3 (Hardcover)
978-1-5255-9382-6 (Paperback)
978-1-5255-9384-0 (eBook)

1. RELIGION, CHRISTIAN LIFE, DEVOTIONAL

Distributed to the trade by The Ingram Book Company

Prayer from the Author

I pray to the Father in the name of Jesus that as you read this Holy-Spirit-filled daily devotional you'll encounter, or re-encounter God through Jesus in a way you've never experienced before, and that your life will be transformed for greatness.

Jesus said, "All things are possible for one who believes"

(Mark 9:23, ESV).

Sharna Knowles

Contents

Dedication		vii
Acknowledgments		ix
Summary		xi
Daily Prayer of Declarations		xiii
1.	Alpha & Omega	1
2.	The Way	3
3.	Salvation through Jesus	5
4.	Holy Spirit Baptism	7
5.	Water Baptism	9
6.	When You Pray!	11
7.	Appointed Time	15
8.	Tempted, but Overcame	17
9.	True Discipleship	19
10.	The Seven Spirits of God	21
11.	Nine Fruits of the Spirit	23
12.	The Life of Giving	25
13.	Hope in God	27

14.	The Church	29
15.	Faith in Action	33
16.	Refuse to Quit	35
17.	The True Vine	37
18.	Fear Not	39
19.	Chosen by God	41
20.	Healer, Deliverer, Restorer	43
21.	Thanksgiving	45
22.	Born to Overcome	47
23.	Power over the Enemy	49
24.	When You Fast	51
25.	The Kingdom of Heaven	55
26.	The Lord's Supper	57
27.	Next Level	59
28.	The Second Coming	61
29.	Victory in Jesus	63
30.	The Great Commission	65

Dedication

This book is dedicated to my late grandmother, Fay Adlin Armstrong.

A woman of God who prayed and cried out to God, interceding on behalf of her children, grandchildren, and others. Though she may seem insignificant to some, she played a great part in making me who I am today.

A homemaker who was a giver, who always cooked enough to share with others or with the less fortunate, who occasionally had extra clothing for those in need, and who took in people from time to time when they needed temporary shelter.

I was super elated when I was officially ordained and graduated on her date of birth, June 1.

Awesome God!

Acknowledgments

This book is inspired and written with instructions from the Holy Spirit. I want to thank God for choosing me to write it. I know that had I not accepted the call to write the book by activating my faith, God would have chosen another person.

To my friend and awesome husband, Charles Knowles, for being a tower of support and giving me advice on the cover design colour—thank you so much, hon.

To my two children, Akeem and Alexis Knowles, for advice on the editor's manuscript evaluation.

To my mother and friend, Olive Armstrong, for the countless prayers, sacrifices, and seeds planted into my life.

To My stepfather, Oneil McFarlane, for his love and support.

To my sister and friend, Tanisha Matthews, for always encouraging me, for helping me with the back-cover picture, from booking the photographer to giving me creative direction on set.

To my nephew Anthony Matthews, you rock.

Thanks to my nine-year-old cousin Hayden Shand for drafting my mock cover design.

Thanks to Carmen Armstrong, Horace Armstrong, and Jennifer Campbell for telling me more than once that they saw books in me. When I started the publishing process, I called Horace and he said, "You write the book yet?" I believe God was speaking through him.

To my Brother Marlon Matthews, The Best is still yet to come.

To Britney Morgan Artistry for always having my makeup on point.

Thanks to my Publisher Michelle Verge and the entire team at FriesenPress.

And Thanks to God once more, as I am elated for such a time as this.

Summary

Grounded in scripture and flowing with encouragement, *30 Days in the Word* is more than just a daily devotional. Beginning with the person of Christ himself and covering the essential points of the gospel, this inspirational offering also provides a concise summary of Christian practice and belief.

Scripture verses, daily reflections, and life applications for every day of the month help to explain, in concise terms, the message of salvation.

This devotional will help you connect passages from scripture to everyday life. It's a straightforward book that presents both the gospel and the beliefs and practices integral to the Christian faith.

Topics such as water baptism, the gifts of the Spirit, fasting, giving, and end times theology are covered to provide an outline of key teachings of the church. It will be a valuable resource for evangelists, discipleship classes, conferences, and high school religious studies reference guide.

Daily Prayer of Declarations
Command Your Day

> Job 38:12
> "Hast thou commanded the morning since thy days; and cause the day-spring to know his place."

> Job 22:28
> "Thou shall also decree a thing, and it shall be established unto thee: and the light shall shine upon thy ways."

I encourage you to take a few minutes each day to say aloud the following declarations before you read the day's devotional.

God spoke this world into existence in Genesis 1:1–3: "And the earth was without form, and void; and darkness was upon the face of the deep. And the Spirit of God moved upon the face of the waters. And God said, Let there be light: and there was light.

As the Spirit of God move upon this book, and as you read and declare, it shall be."

In Genesis 1:26, God gives us dominion over the fish of the sea, and over the air, and over the cattle, and over every creeping thing that creeps upon the earth. Declare it and walk into it; faith without works is dead.

As you read for the next thirty days, declaring and believing, you will experience changes for good. Utilize these words like daily living food and medicine.

1. "I am forgiven…" 1 John 1:9

2. "I am set free…" John 8:36.

3. "I am healed…" Isaiah 53:5.

4. "I am whole…" Mark 5:34.

5. "I am blessed…" Deuteronomy 28:3–5.

6. "I am victorious in Christ…" 1 Corinthians 15:57.

7. "I am favored with God and man…" Proverbs 3:4.

8. "I am beautiful and wonderfully made…" Psalm 139:14.

9. "I am the head and not the tail…" Deuteronomy 28:13.

10. "I am blessed going out and coming in…" Deuteronomy 28:6.

11. "I am divinely covered and protected by God…" Psalm 91.

12. "I am a winner, an overcomer, and I am more than a conqueror…" Romans 8:37–39.

13. "My gifts will make room for me and bring me before great people…" Proverbs 18:16.

14. "My best years are ahead of me, and my latter shall be greater…" Haggai 2:9.

15. "My coast and territories are enlarged…" 1 Chronicles 4:10.

16. "I shall not lack any good thing…" Psalm 34:10.

17. "I shall be in health and prosper in all things…" 3 John 2.

18. "I shall be unmoveable, unshakeable, and unstoppable…" 1 Corinthians 15:58.

19. "I shall eat the good of this land…" Isaiah 1:19.

20. "I shall not die but live to declare God's work…" Psalm 118:17.

21. "I will be celebrated…" Psalm 149:5.

22. "I will fulfil my God-given purpose…" Revelation 17:17.

23. "I walk by faith and not by sight…" 2 Corinthians 5:7.

24. "When I pray, God will answer me according to his will…" 1 John 5:14–15.

25. "The Lord will fight my battles and I shall be at peace…" Exodus 14:14.

26. "All things are working together for my good…" Romans 8:28.

27. "His grace is sufficient for me; his mercies are new daily…" Lamentation 3:22–23.

28. "Overflow and abundance shall be my portion…" Psalm 23:5.

29. "Those who rise up against me shall flee several ways before my face…" Deuteronomy 28:7.

30. "I have been restored…" Joel 2:25.

Day One
Alpha & Omega

Scripture: John 1:1–8

John begins Jesus's story not from his birth, but from the beginning with God as the Word of God, as the creator and the true light of the world. The purpose of the book of John is to reach the non-Christian world; therefore, it's a great book for new converts as well.

> John 10:30
> Jesus declares, "I and my father are one."
>
> Revelation 1:8
> "I am Alpha and Omega, the beginning and the ending, saith the Lord, which is, and which was, and which is to come, the Almighty."

Today's Reflection
Start and end your day with God, giving thanks and praises unto him, commanding your day daily. Try this for the next thirty days, and your life will never be the same.

Day Two

The Way

Scripture: John 3:1–21

Many are still to this day asking the question, Who is Jesus?

Even John the Baptist that introduced him as the word and the beginning later asked Jesus if he should look for another.

The Samaritan woman at the well called him a Jew, then a prophet, and then later wondered if he was the Messiah. The Roman governor wondered if he was the King of the Jews, and the Jewish leaders said he was from the devil.

God revealed to Peter that he (Jesus) was the Messiah, the Son of the living God, and Peter declared that in Matthew 16:16.

One of Jesus's disciples, Thomas, asked Jesus how he could know the way. Jesus answered him in John 14:6 by saying, "I am the way, the truth, and the life: no man cometh unto the Father, but by me."

The only way to God is through Jesus.

He is:

1. **The way**. There is a right and a wrong way—two ways of life. In Matthew 7:13–14, Jesus makes it clear through a parable that the wide gate leads to destruction, and the narrow gate leads to life.

2. **The truth**. There is the truth, and there are lies. In John 8:44, Jesus says that the devil is the father of lies.

3. **The life**. In John 3:16, Jesus states that God so loved the world that he gave his son for us to have eternal life.

Today's Reflection

Jesus, the way, the truth, and the life!

Know who you are and stand firm, focusing on your goals, mission, and purpose. Press on to the end. Rise above the doubters, critics, accusers, and even the unsure. Don't waste precious time trying to prove who you are, even to family and friends; otherwise, you'll become frustrated, depressed, and anxious.

God has given you the spirit of love, power, and a sound mind.

Don't allow yourself to be rerouted and derailed. Better is the end of a thing than the beginning thereof.

Jesus knew who he was and endured to the end. You too can endure to the end if you don't lose the heart.

Day Three
Salvation through Jesus

Scripture: John 20:31

> But these are written, that ye might believe that Jesus is the Christ, the Son of God; and that believing ye might have life through his name.

Have you accepted Jesus Christ as Lord and Savior of your life?

Here's How:
If you believe with your heart and declare that Jesus is Lord with your mouth, then you are saved. It's as simple as that.

> Romans 10:9–10
> It's with your mouth that you profess and with your heart that you believe that God raised Jesus from the dead.

Salvation Prayer

Lord Jesus, I'm a sinner. I believe that you died on the cross for me and that you shed your precious blood for the forgiveness of my sins. I believe that on the third day, you rose from the dead. I accept you now as my Savior and my Lord.

> Luke 15:10
> The angels are rejoicing
>
> 2 Corinthians 5:17
> The old has gone, the new has come

Today's Reflection

As you embark in your new relationship with God through Jesus Christ, many blessings are made available to you, including everlasting life.

> John 3:16
> "For God so love the world, that he gave his only begotten Son, that whosoever believeth in him should not perish, but have everlasting life.

Day Four

Holy Spirit Baptism

Scripture: John 14:26

> "But the Comforter, which is the Holy Ghost, whom the Father will send in my name, he shall teach you all things, and bring all things to your remembrance…"

Who is the Holy Spirit?
He will teach you all things and bring back all things to your remembrance. He's the third person in the Trinity, which consists of Father, Son, and Holy Spirit.

What is the baptism of the Holy Spirit?
It is for every believer in the Lord Jesus Christ; it's a promise gift that every believer should seek after with earnest faith until they receive this promised blessing, as written in Acts 2:38–39.

In Luke 24:49, Jesus tells his apostles to wait and tarry until they receive the baptism of the Holy Spirit. Without it, they will be like a ship without a rudder—useless, with no power.

We live in the age of the spirits, and we need the Spirit of God to override and overshadow all other spirits.

> 1 Corinthians 12:1
> "Now concerning spiritual gifts, brethren, I would not have you ignorant."

The baptism of the Holy Spirit is identified by the initial physical sign of speaking in tongue as the Spirit gives utterance; however, the evidence may not appear on the same day. This is why Jesus told his apostles to *tarry* until they received it.

As you continue to abide in him, you will receive the promised gift.

Receive the baptism of the Holy Spirit by praying and receiving, not coaching. It is a gift from God.

Receiving the Baptism of the Holy Spirit Prayer
Father, in the matchless name of Jesus I receive your promised gift of the Holy Spirit to lead, guide, direct, and empower me.

Baptize me now with your Holy Spirit and let your Spirit enables me to live an overcomer's life here on earth. Let me be a partaker in heaven. Amen.

Today's Reflection
The evidence of speaking in tongues may not manifest the same day; however, continue to worship, praise, pray, and abide in the Word, and you will see the manifestation of the promised gift.

Day Five

Water Baptism

Scripture: Matthew 28:18–20

"Go ye therefore, and teach all nations, baptizing them in the name of the Father, and of the Son, and of the Holy Ghost" (v.19).

Water baptism is the outward symbol of what has already transpired in the heart for full salvation. Baptism is administered by immersing in water and baptizing in the name of the Father, Son, and Holy Spirit in obedience to the Great Commission in Matthew 28:19.

Water baptism comes after you accept Jesus as Lord and Savior of your life. In Acts 2:41, those who gladly received the Word were baptized the same day. In Acts 16:33, the Philippian jailor was converted and baptized straightaway. In other words, as soon as you're are able to, you should be baptized. Do not put it off. Jesus was baptized as an example in Matthew 3:13,17.

Today's Reflection
You don't need lessons or classes before water baptism. Once you've accepted Jesus as Lord and Savior, water baptism should take place as soon as possible; however, new converts' classes or lessons can follow afterwards.

Day Six

When You Pray!

Scripture: Luke 6:12–19

> "And it came to pass in those days, that he went out into a mountain to pray, and continued all night in prayer to God" (v. 12).

The greatest power on earth is prayer. Jesus said in Luke 10:19, "Behold, I give unto you power to tread on serpents and scorpions, and over all the power of the enemy…" This means the enemy has power as well, but the power of God overpowers every other power. God's power never fades.

Prayer is vital and fulfils every promise. Paul writes in 2 Corinthians 1:20 that all the promises of God in him are yea and Amen.

Prayer brings the power of God alive. In scripture, Jesus prays all night, and the power of God comes alive through healing, deliverance, miracles, feeding, teachings. and preaching.

As he taught his disciples, he said, "When ye pray" (Matthew 6:7), which means prayer is *mandatory* and *vital*.

Daniel prayed and was delivered from the lions. Hannah was barren and she prayed, and God opened her womb and gave her a son, Samuel, one of the major prophets in the Bible. The Hebrew boys prayed, and they were delivered from the fiery furnace.

I've seen the mighty hand of God move on my behalf several times, and things that were impossible became possible. God can and will do the same for you as well.

One of several miracles I've received from God occurred when one of my mother's friends diagnosed with a cancer that had spread. The doctors told her that there was nothing else they could do and pronounced that she would only live for a few days. I came in prayer and agreement for healing and long life. It has been over thirteen years now, and she is cancer-free and living a joyful life today.

Another supernatural miracle I received from God came for my daughter Alexis, who had bronchial asthma. This caused periodic attacks of coughing, wheezing, shortness of breath, and tightness in the chest. She often needed a chamber and three puffers.

One day when she was about six years old, I sat her on the kitchen counter and started praying for her. At the end of the prayer, she lifted her two hands to Heaven and said, "Mom. I am healed in Jesus's name!" From that day on, she has been healed and set free from that spirit of infirmity.

Alexis is nineteen years old today. She has anchored in many relays in high school, was the MVP in track and field, won the Coaches' Award, and more. Alexis has been healthy since that day and is a second-year university student in Medical Science. Miracle-working God and Alexis believed.

> "... all things are possible to him that believeth" (Mark 9:23b).

Today's Reflection

Start and end your day with prayer! Daniel prayed three times a day and was undefeated. The psalmist said, "Let the morning bring me word from your unfailing love, for I have put my trust in you" (Psalm 143:8, NIV).

Start where you are. Five minutes per day this week, ten minutes per day next week, with consistency and dedication, God will intervene. Soon, you'll be praying throughout the night.

Napoleon Hill said, "The man that masters himself through self- discipline can never be mastered by others." Discipline yourself to pray and let it become your breakfast, lunch, and dinner.

When your foundation is prayer, you become unmovable, unshakeable, unstoppable, and even untouchable by people. God himself would need to remove that hedge of protection from you.

Day Seven

Appointed Time

Scripture: John 2:1–4

> "Jesus saith unto her … mine hour is not yet come" (v. 4).

To everything there is a time and season, there is night and day, summer and winter, seed and harvest time. There is also an appointed time for you. God's plan for you is to prosper you and to give you an expected end. Cultivate good seeds, and you will reap a harvest.

There's also a preparation time. It takes obedience, sacrifice, dedication, discipline, practice, and staying in God's will.

If you're not where you want to be in serving God, or even in your personal life, there's no time like today to rearrange your priorities. Know your gifts and talents, and as you spend time in the process, they will make room for you.

We are a product of our time. Jesus spent hours praying so that he could see the miracles when it was his time. This is true of athletes, doctors, pastors, farmers, or whatever field you're in. There's an appointed time for you.

Today's Reflection
Don't operate out of your time or season. It can lead to fruitlessness, spiritual death, detour, and even untimely death. Run your own race; stay in your own lane. Don't compare your life's journey with another person's. Comparison will steal your joy, peace, and time.

The only gift we all have in common is the gift of time. We all have twenty-four hours in any given day, so use your time wisely.

Ms. Crawford, my grade four teacher, stated: "If you fail to prepare, then you already prepare to fail."

Jesus had an appointed time to fulfil his purpose here on earth before he was showcased.

From the time I was twenty-seven years of age, I had a goal to write my first book and have it launched for my thirtieth birthday. Over fifteen years later, I believe this is my divinely appointed time to write my first book, divinely inspired by the Holy Spirit.

Day Eight

Tempted, but Overcame

Scripture: Matthew 4:1–17

> "Then saith Jesus unto him, Get thee hence, Satan: for it is written, Thou shalt worship the Lord thy God, and him only shalt thou serve" (v. 10).

Just before Jesus began his ministry, the devil came to him not just once, but three times. Jesus used the Word to overcome every one of the devil's schemes. Remember, the devil also used the Word from scriptures. The devil is the father of lies (John 8:44), but you too can overcome the traps and schemes of the tempter by using the Word.

Today's Reflection
Clothe yourself with the Word of God and abide in him, as he will abide in you.

Sometimes things will present themselves and look glorious in many enticing ways. They'll look attractive and tempting, but remember to test the spirit, as the devil knows the Word as well.

Day Nine
True Discipleship

Scripture: Matthew 7:21

> "Not everyone that saith unto me, Lord, Lord, shall enter into the Kingdom of Heaven; but he that doeth the will of my Father which is in heaven."

There is a price to pay to be a true disciple of God through Jesus Christ: time, dedication, love, and sacrifice. Who is a disciple? Someone who believes in Jesus and seeks to follow him in his or her daily life.

Originally, a disciple/apostle was someone who literally knew Jesus in the flesh and followed him, but after he was taken into Heaven, anyone who was committed to Jesus was called a disciple/apostle (see Mark 16:19–20).

Anyone can say they're a Christian, but not everyone is committed to Jesus Christ. Sitting in a sanctuary on your day of worship doesn't qualify you to be a disciple; rather, you must have the mind and heart of Christ (Matthew 16:24–26).

We are all called to be disciples and use our God-given talents and gifts to fulfil our purpose, but too often the problem is we want our brothers' and sisters' gifts and talents.

In Genesis 37:1–11, Joseph told his brothers his dream, and they were able to interpret it, but they were so focused on Joseph's future that they missed the fact that they had the gift of interpretation.

With social media at our fingertips, we can evangelize anytime, anywhere.

Today's Reflection

Taking up our cross daily means being selfless. It won't be easy some days, but surrendering your day over to God every morning will give you peace.

God promised that he would be with you always, even to the end (Matthew 28:20).

At times you'll be rejected, laughed at, heartbroken, accused, knocked down, and the list goes on. Don't be distracted; stay focused. There's joy in doing God's will, and he will supply all your needs. True discipleship comes with a price and no deficit, but there are *two guaranteed rewards.*

- When you seek first the Kingdom of God and all his righteousness, all your needs will be taken care of here on earth (Matthew 6:33).

- You will receive eternal life for doing God's will (Matthew 7:21).

Day Ten

The Seven Spirits of God

Scripture: Isaiah 11:2–3

> "And the Spirit of the Lord shall rest upon him, the spirit of wisdom and understanding, the spirit of counsel and might, the spirit of knowledge and of the fear of the Lord; And shall make him of quick understanding in the fear of the Lord: and he shall not judge after the sight of his eyes, neither reprove after the hearing of his ears."

There are two realms: spirit and flesh. The Word of God is profitable and will equip, teach, instruct, and bring correction.

In order to be successful in our daily living, we must let the seven Spirits of God rest upon us and walk in them.

Wisdom: Ephesians 5:15–16 tells us to walk upright, not as a fool, but as the wise, because the days are evil.

Understanding: We ought to trust in the Lord with all our heart and lean not on our own understanding (Proverbs 3:5).

Counsel: Many are the counsel in a man's heart; however, only God's counsel shall stand (Proverbs 19:21).

Might/Power: Jesus called the twelve together and gave them power and authority over all the demons and to heal diseases (Luke 9:1).

Knowledge: The fear of the Lord is the beginning of knowledge (Proverbs 1:7)

The Fear of the Lord: The fear of the Lord will prolong life, but the years of the wicked will be shortened (Proverbs 10:27).

Spirit of God: The Spirit of the lord is upon me, because the Lord has anointed me to bring the good news to the afflicted, he has sent me to bind up the broken hearted, to proclaim liberty to the captives and freedom to prisoners... Luke 4:18 paraphrased.

Today's Reflection:
God's Spirit does the work. Walk in the seven Spirits of God.

Day Eleven
Nine Fruits of the Spirit

Scripture: John 15:2

> Every branch in me that bears no fruit,
> he taketh away.

The fruits of the Spirit are visible attributes of the Christian life. Galatian 5:22–25 lists the nine fruits of the Spirit: love, joy, peace, long suffering (yes, long suffering), gentleness, goodness, faithfulness, meekness, and self-control. These are all attributes that we should be producing as born-again Christians.

As all nine come to perfection, you'll be more fruitful and effective in your daily walk, especially if you're leading, ministering, and evangelizing. Your light *must* shine, and it will be evident based on the fruits you bear. Jesus said, "Ye shall know them by their fruits" (Matthew 7:16).

You can also read Galatians 5:19–21, which describes the works of the flesh and how they manifest. I'll touch briefly on the works of the flesh, which work in opposition to the fruits of the Spirit. The works of the flesh will *manifest* adultery, fornication, uncleanness, lasciviousness, idolatry, witchcraft, hatred, variance, emulations, wrath, strife, sedition, heresies, envying, murders, drunkenness, and revelling. The Word of God states that such works will not see the Kingdom of God.

Today's Reflection
As you abide in God by reading the Word daily, praying, giving thanks, praising, and fasting when you can, you will walk in the Spirit naturally and the Spirit of the Lord will rest upon you, as read in Day 10.

Day Twelve
The Life of Giving

Scripture: Proverbs 11:24 (ESV)

> One gives freely, yet grows all the richer;
> another withholds what he should give,
> and only suffers want.

Giving evokes gratitude and will have a positive affect on your mental well-being. I'm not talking about giving out of compulsion, reluctantly, or under pressure. I'm talking about cheerfully giving from the heart while walking in the wisdom of God (see 2 Corinthians 9:6–7).

You will never be able to out-give God. I could write this entire book on giving and how the Lord continually supplies my every need in all areas. When you live a life of giving, God will take your two fishes and five loaves and use them to make up every difference in your life.

Sometimes experiencing God's continual blessings on your life will offend people. Instead of asking for your formula, some people might become jealous and envious.

Giving comes from the heart and will determine your way of living. You'll never live in lack when you're a true giver.

My grandmother, Fay Armstrong, was a true giver, and my mother, Olive Armstrong, lives the life of giving and is blessed with God's favor.

When you give to the poor, the less fortunate, or those in a time of need, you lend to God (Proverbs 19:17).

When my son was about seven years old, he looked at me and said, "Mom, you know you'll never be rich."

I asked, "Why, baby?"

"Because everything you have you give away."

"No, baby. I'm rich in God through health, family, and peace of mind. The Lord always supplies our needs according to his riches, as he owns the heaven and the earth. When you walk in the principles and laws of God, you can rest and know that his Word is yes and Amen."

Currently, my son is a faithful giver, giving back in several ways.

Today's Reflection

Live a balanced, fulfilled life; seek God first and his righteousness; give your time; help a cause; volunteer when you can; give a smile; and give with love.

I volunteered in a seniors' home for over seven years with eighty-nine-year-old Elsie, which was so precious and priceless. In one of her last conversations with me, she said, "Sharna, when you started you were a volunteer, then you became a friend, and now you're family." That's priceless. There are many ways you can give. Give where your heart and passion are. Live the life of giving.

Day Thirteen
Hope in God

Scripture: Isaiah 40:31 (NIV)

> … those who hope in the Lord will renew their strength. They will soar on wings like eagles; they will run and not grow weary, they will walk and not faint.

Have you ever felt like you were going around in circles, or that you were trapped in the day? Alone? Unsure? Ever felt like giving up? Like nobody understood or even cared at times? Has your heart been crushed? Are you constantly misunderstood? Unappreciated? Underestimated? The list definitely goes on. If this speaks to you today, I would love to encourage you that there is hope in God. He is near to those who call on him, and he is always a present help in time of need. Call on him, and he will deliver you. When you feel down and out, call on the name of Jesus, and you shall be delivered, healed, and set free. With people it's impossible, but with God all things are possible (see Matthew 19:26).

If you are breathing, there is still hope. You can laugh again, run again, dance again, and dream again. He is a big God; he is the God of all humanity. Nothing is too hard for him, and nothing is hidden from his eyes. God is greater than any problem you can face. Hold onto this promised scripture in Jeremiah 17:7–8: "Blessed are those whose hope and trust is in God … even in time of drought they will be taken care of." Paraphrased.

I have been in situations where I felt like all hope was lost and there was no way out. I cried out to God, and he made ways, and he used me in those situations to minister to others.

Don't give up. God have a purpose for your pain. God can make a way in the wilderness, and a river in the deserts (Isaiah 43:19).

Today's Reflection

Let God go before you and level every mountain. Don't get anxious or worry about anything, but in everything make all your requests known to God, giving him thanks and knowing that you will find peace in him, as he is able to do more than you can imagine or ask.

Nothing is impossible with him.

Day Fourteen
The Church

Scripture: Matthew 16:18

Jesus is the rock that the church is built on. He purchased the church with his own blood (Acts 20:28). The church isn't a building. The building is a place of assembly, and we are not to forsake the assembly, as it helps us to exhort one another while preparing for the second coming (see Hebrews 10:24–25). You and I are the church. Jesus is the rock in us as we continue to abide in him as he does in us.

Many look solely to their church attendance to meet their needs, so their attitude is that the ministry is there to serve them. At times, they will hop from ministry to ministry, running after prophet this and prophetess that while looking for a word. Some believe they can purchase a miracle. They run after person and don't seek first the Kingdom of God and all his righteousness, so that God can add all that they need unto them.

Jesus is the Word. We know God by spending time in the Word according to scripture, praying without ceasing, fasting, and praising and worshipping him through Jesus Christ. Don't get me wrong—God uses his prophets and men and women of God to bring forth his Word, to set free, comfort, warn, heal, and bring correction and instruction in right living (Jeremiah 1:10).

We also live in an age when the church lacks prayer, and our ears are itching. People are clinging to soothsaying and the spirit of divination and are rejecting sound doctrine that comes from God's Word. At times we see men and women of God blinded by the Jezebel and familiar spirits that have bombarded the body of Christ and bound leaders. Acts 16:16–24 records that Paul and Silas rebuked the spirit of divination out of a damsel. They were called troublemakers, beaten, jailed, and shackled for doing God's work.

In 2 Timothy 4:2–5, Paul wrote that we ought to preach the Word of God in and out of season to reprove, rebuke, and exhort with all longsuffering and doctrine. For we see that the time has come when the saints are not enduring sound doctrine but are going after their own lusts and heaping to themselves their own teachers. Having itching ears, they're turning their ears from the truth, and they shall be turned into fables. However, we must watch in all things, endure afflictions, do the work of an evangelist, and make full proof of the ministry.

Many platforms have become stages for performances, self-edification, and people-pleasing to keep the crowd entertained. But they don't invite a real encounter with God.

First and foremost, we attend services to worship God: giving him thanks, praise, and adoration. At times during worship, healing, deliverance, breakthroughs, and miracles will come. It's also a time to receive instructions regarding the principles and laws of God.

Loving the preacher will motivate some to attend special services, but those who attend all services, such as mid-week Bible study and prayer services, attend for the love of God.

Today's Reflection

Take the church with you always, wherever you go, and share the good news that "For God so love the world, that he gave his only begotten Son, that whosoever believeth in him should not perish, but have everlasting life (John 3:16).

Let your light so shine before men so they can glorify God.

Day Fifteen

Faith in Action

Scripture: John 5:1–9

Jesus healed the impotent man by telling him to arise, take up his bed and walk.

Many times, we're stuck at the same place because we refuse to arise, change our mindset or inherited patterns, and reposition ourselves.

At times, we play the blame game, as did the man in the scripture at the pool of Bethesda.

It's my mother's, it's my father's, it's my sister's, or it's my brother's fault. But it's never too late for healing, deliverance, breakthrough, or restoration, even if you're in that situation for thirty-eight years.

Put faith into action and do what you were born to do. "For as the body without the spirit is dead, so faith without works is dead also" (James 2:26).

Today's Reflection
Be confident that if you have faith as small as a mustard seed, you can speak to the biggest of mountains and it shall be moved. Put your faith into action and arise today.

Write the book, arise and be healed, be delivered, be free, start that business, start eating healthy, start working towards buying that home, arise and break the inherited family pattern that's not aligned with your God-given purpose and destiny. Your best years are still ahead of you, your latter shall be greater than your past, and your best is yet to come. Arise and make it happen.

Day Sixteen

Refuse to Quit

Scripture: Galatians 6:9

> "And let us not be weary in well doing: for in due season we shall reap, if we faint not."

In his final year as a student athlete in university, after having four head coaches in five years of playing football, my son Akeem was somewhat tired and almost quit. I told him that quitters never win, and winners never quit. Months after that intense conversation, he went on to thank me that he hadn't quit, and now he's an alumnus completing both football and his studies. Do not give up! Do not stop! Do not quit! Complete your purpose.

God can't go back on his words, and he who started a good thing in you is able to complete it. Don't give up on your marriage, dreams, hopes, business, purpose, school, or even that sport that you've been called and chosen for. God's plan for you is to prosper you and give you an expected end.

You can defy all odds and limitations. Dr. Adolf Brown states: "Do not judge an end, or a finish by the beginning."

Even Jesus—Light of the World, King of Kings, Alpha and Omega, Righteous One, Savior, Great High Priest—started out in a manger, but he didn't belong there so his destiny didn't end there. Jesus had to go through the process, as do you and I.

In Luke 22:41–42, Jesus prayed to the Father to remove the cup from him, as he knew it was an unbearable task, but he continued and pray the Father's will. Endure to the end and pray the Father's will for your life.

Many billion-dollar companies start out in a basement or garage with almost little to nothing. You can do it also. Press on, even though you may be judged, laughed at, wrongfully accused, hated, lied on, ridiculed, and copied. Keep moving! You can overcome. John 16:33 is a scripture of promise, stating that you can find true peace in God, as in the world there are always trials and tribulations.

Today's Reflection
You will never produce if you quit. Failure loves comfort, so get out of your comfort zone and win. At times it might seems painful or difficult, but you will reap if you don't lose heart.

Day Seventeen
The True Vine

Scripture: John 15:1–17

Jesus! The true vine.

Abide in him, and he will abide in you.

Take refuge in God, for he is a tower where no enemy can reach you.

In your day of trouble, he is able to hide you. In the fear of the Lord there is strong confidence, and his children will have refuge. When the storms of life come, let him be your defence. God is always a very present help in time of need. Even when we fall short, he is able to forgive and cleanse us of all our unrighteousness. His Word states that if you abide in him, you will ask anything, and it shall be yours.

Today's Reflection

Jesus is the vine, and you are the branches. Abide in him, and he will abide in you.

Day Eighteen
Fear Not

Scripture: 1 Samuel 17:23–37

When God is on your side, you have nothing to fear but the fear of God himself. David feared not, because he knew the God he served. He knew God had delivered him from the bears and the lions; he knew he served a victorious God, the one who has never lost a battle to this day, the God before whom angels bow. Heaven and earth adore him; he is the king of kings, the conquering lion of the tribe of Judea. David knew that God was his battle fighter. He is the God who owns the heavens and the earth and everything in it. David knew that God had sent the prophet Samuel to anoint him for a purpose, even when others couldn't see.

As David inquired about Goliath's challenge, vs 26-30, he didn't get distracted with Eliab's comments and innuendos; instead, he turned to the other side with confidence and spoke the very same words. They reached the right person, and David went on to attain victory over Goliath. Stay focused. Ignore the innuendos and comments birthed from jealousy.

Today's Reflection

David was focused. He didn't allow Eliab's insecurities to distract him from what God had anointed him for. Don't get distracted with small stuff when Goliath is the target. Fear not! Focus! God is with you; he will not leave you or forsake you. David said, "Yea, thou I walk through the valley of the shadow of death, I will fear no evil: for thou art with me" (Psalm 23:4a).

Be confident that God is with you and fear not!

Day Nineteen

Chosen by God

Scripture: 1 Samuel 16:7

> "But the Lord said to Samuel, 'Do not consider his appearance or his height, for I have rejected him. The Lord does not look at the things people look at. People look at the outward appearance, but the Lord looks at the heart.'"

While people will look at our outer appearances, stature, titles, and at times credentials, God examines the heart. Only God can search the heart. You may often be judged by what is visible to the natural sight, which includes your attire, physique, race, ethnicity, age, and gender.

Read 1 Samuel 16:1–13. When God sent the prophet Samuel to the house of Jesse to anoint one of his sons king, even the man of God who was sent from God with detailed instructions got into his own self and intellect and assumed Eliab was the Lord's anointed. But the Lord told Samuel not to look at outward appearances. Even David's father didn't consider him to be king material. David wasn't invited to the sacrifice or the anointing service like the other brothers.

God refused all the brothers that seems to fit the part in the sight of man.

Often a man or woman of God will get a word and be sent by God, but it's the right word but the wrong person. Right word, wrong brother as we saw in scripture. Can you imagine what would have happened had Samuel anointed Eliab King?

Today's Reflection
Live a life that's pleasing to God. Be a person after God's own heart.

Be confident in who God has anointed you to become, especially when the naysayers say, "Oh he's just a shepherd boy; he's only the carpenter's son; she's just the cleaner; she's just the cook; he's a high school dropout; nothing good comes from that city." Be bold and courageous. Don't fear what people think or see. If God has chosen and selected you, it doesn't matter who has rejected you. God's plans outweigh everything.

Day Twenty
Healer, Deliverer, Restorer

Scripture: Matthew 4:23–25 (NIV)

Jesus went throughout Galilee, teaching in their synagogues, proclaiming the good news of the kingdom, and healing every disease and sickness among the people. News about him spread all over Syria, and people brought to him all who were ill with various diseases, those suffering severe pain, the demon-possessed, those having seizures, and the paralysed; and he healed them. Large crowds from Galilee, the Decapolis, Jerusalem, Judea and the region across the Jordan followed him.

Jesus went about healing, feeding, teaching, and preaching while setting the captives free. When Jesus is your foundation, you will experience open Heaven here on Earth.

At the age of ten, shortly after I'd given my life over to God and accepted water baptism, I had a spirit of infirmity. The doctors claimed it was an issue with the brain. I remember my grandmother crying out to God in the name of Jesus, and I was healed from that day. Awesome God indeed. I have experienced the mighty hand of God through healing, deliverance, and restoration. God has also used me through Jesus to pray for the sick and set them free as they believe. The Lord has anointed me with the gift of healing and transformation.

Today's Reflection
God is near to those who call on him. Call on him, and he will heal, deliver, and restore you.

Day Twenty-One
Thanksgiving

Scripture: Psalm 106:1 (NIV)

> Give thanks to the Lord for he is good;
> his love endures forever.

Give thanks always and for all things to God the Father in the name of our Lord Jesus Christ.

Paul and Silas gave thanks and sang praises to God while shackled in the dungeon for actually doing good, and God delivered them. Thanksgiving and praise activate the mighty move of God.

In every situation and circumstance, give thanks. God will intervene and make every crooked path straight, part the Red Sea, and bring down every stubborn wall, and you shall rejoice with great testimony.

Today's Reflection
Give thanks always and at all times. Live a life of thanksgiving.

Day Twenty-Two

Born to Overcome

Scripture: Isaiah 46:10

> "I make known the end from the beginning, from ancient times, what is still to come. I say, 'My purpose will stand, and I will do all that I please.'"

If you are called to a particular area, field, career, or ministry, and you've been rejected directly or indirectly, don't give up or lose heart. Know who you are and know your purpose. Don't let anyone determine who you are by how they view you.

How you feel about yourself is more important than how people see you, because people will treat you according to how they view you. If they view you as not called or chosen in a particular area or position, they'll treat you that way. Rise above that! Focus! Keep your eyes on the prize!

The Spirit of the Lord was upon Jesus to teach, heal, deliver, set captives free, and preach the Kingdom of God, yet he was rejected even in his own town, because they viewed him as just the carpenter's son. He overcame the rejection and so can you by focusing on your vision, dreams, mission, goals, and purpose. Jesus overcame because he knew his purpose and mission. Sometimes you know who you are but others around you don't.

Rowan Atkinson was rejected by many TV shows due to his stammering problem. He overcame by starting his own show, *Mr. Bean,* which became a global success. People will put their own diagnostics on you when they don't know your calling and purpose. Know that you are able, even when others see you as incapable.

Today's Reflection
Know who you are and whose you are and walk into what you are called to do or become. Know that when people reject you, you are elected by God.

Plant it! Do it! Live it!

Day Twenty-Three
Power over the Enemy

Scripture: Luke 10:17–19

Even the devil is subjected to us through the name of Jesus. Every knee shall bow, and every tongue must confess that Jesus Christ is Lord.

As children of the highest God, we have the power to tread on serpents and scorpions and over all the power of the enemy according to scriptures. The word is power, food, and life. The enemy is not flesh and blood but rather the invisible forces working behind the scenes and manifesting in a body.

We must deal with spiritual things in the spirit. If you fight a spiritual war in the natural, you'll lose every time and continue to go around in circles feeling frustrated, depressed, and bound. This will often lead to destiny redirection, and serious deliverance is a must. The enemy only comes to rob, kill, steal, and destroy. Use the power that has been given to you, which is prayer and fasting. Walk in the wisdom of God and pray for the gift of discernment, as it's vital in the last days in which we're living—the age of the spirits.

Today's Reflection

Utilize the power given to you in every area of your life through the Word of God. Jesus used the Word to defeat the devil in Matthew 4:1–12. Do not be ignorant of his devices, lest you perish.

Day Twenty-Four
When You Fast

Scripture: Matthew 6:16

Fasting is vital for the believer in God through Jesus.

We see many nonbelievers fast for many other reasons, including medical.

Jesus taught about "when you fast," not "if you fast." Jesus fasted, as did Elijah, Esther, Anna, Moses, David, and many others. Fasting empowers, break chains, shackles, revives, and helps to overcome challenges.

In Matthew 17:21, Jesus said that some things only go when you add fasting to prayer. Esther called for three days fasting and prayer to save her people from death, and God delivered. They obtained victory over the enemy. Fasting is unto God, not unto man.

Isaiah 58:3–4 addresses the human way of fasting. In the day of fasting, some people still find pleasures. They fast for strife and debate, to smite wickedness, to make their voices heard on high, and to look holier than thou. Jesus called these people "hypocrites." In Matthew 6:16, he states: "They have their reward."

God's Way of Fasting
Isaiah 58:5–12
We are to go to God with self-denial, humbling ourselves, and bowing down to him.

V. 7 Give to the poor and needy.

V. 8 Your health shall spring forth speedily, and the Glory of God shall be your reward. What an assurance!

V. 9 When you call, God will answer; when you cry, he shall say, "Here I am!"

In 2005, two years after purchasing our second home, my husband and I ran into difficulty with the mortgage payments. We came home one day to a twenty-four-hours notice to vacate—it was that far gone. Instead of getting anxious, we agreed to an immediate emergency fasting and prayer night, calling and crying out to God, and God delivered. We went on to live in that home for eleven more years and sold it with profitable gain. Awesome God indeed!

V. 10 Your light shall rise in obscurity, and any darkness in your life shall flee; you shall be as bright as the noon day.

V. 11 The Lord will guide you continually and provide for you in times of drought.

Today's Reflection
Fasting is mandatory for every believer in Christ. It's God's secret weapon. Jesus said that some things only go when you add fasting to your prayers to loosen bands of wickedness, undo heavy burdens, let the oppressed go free,

and break the yoke of bondage (see Isaiah 58:6). When you add fasting to prayer, you'll be rooted and grounded in your purpose and destiny.

Sometimes we're pregnant with purpose for too long, going around in circles. Fast and pray to repair the breach and raise up foundations of many generations (see Isaiah 58:12).

Day Twenty-Five
The Kingdom of Heaven

Scripture: Matthew 4:17

As Jesus's ministry began, he preached the Kingdom of Heaven, not himself. He is the way to the Kingdom of Heaven. Jesus taught that not everyone will enter this kingdom, just those who do the will of God.

It's good to do a self-assessment of where you are with God and what fruits you're producing. Align yourself with God's will for your life. Know what on earth you're here for. Rick Warren's *What on Earth Am I Here For?* is a good book to read. We often get caught up in doing our will and not the will of God.

Today's Reflection
Are you doing your will or God's will for your life? It's never too late to evaluate and reset.

Day Twenty-Six
The Lord's Supper

Scripture: Luke 22:19–20

> "And he took bread, and gave thanks, and brake it, and gave unto them, saying, This is my body which is given for you: this do in remembrance of me" (v. 19).

We can partake in the Lord's Supper as often as possible in remembrance of his body that was bruised. The bread represents his body, while the liquid represents his blood that was shed for remission of sin. By his stripes we can declare healing… Isaiah 53:5

We ought to examine our hearts according to scriptures and not partake in the Lord's Supper unworthily (1 Corinthians 11:29).

Repentance is necessary according to 1 John 1:9.

Today's Reflection
Jesus paid it all in full on the cross; because of that, you can overcome the issues of life.

Whom Jesus sets free is free indeed—free from guilt, condemnation, addictions, fear, anxiety, sickness, and unforgiveness.

God's promises according to Proverbs 4:22 are life to those who find them and healing to their entire body.

1 Kings 8:56 reveals that God has not failed one of his promises.

Day Twenty-Seven

Next Level

Scripture: 1 Corinthians 16:9

> "For a great door and effectual is opened unto me, and there are many adversaries."

Wherever there's a new level or a great door, there are many adversaries. There will be many opposing forces, as evil is always chasing after good. At times, new levels come with bigger obstacles, barriers, trials, tribulations, and loneliness.

I knew many years ago that I had to write my first book. Year in and year out, I thought of several names for my book. At the Called Leaders conference in Denver, Colorado, Pastor Touré Roberts mentioned two things that can take us to the next level sometimes: "Writing a book and finding a destiny connector." I knew without a doubt that this was it for me. Right after that, the Lord started downloading the information for this book non-stop.

I felt like I'd been pregnant for far too long. The moment this manuscript was completed, I felt as if I'd given birth to quadruplets.

A huge load came off, and I felt joy and release. I believe I have birthed Purpose and Destiny. I hope that as you read this devotional, you're already on your way to greatness. Read and recommend this book to your family and friends.

The new level will require:

1. Praying without ceasing (1 Thessalonians 5:17).

2. Praying always to the Father in the name of Jesus (1 Timothy 2:5). Jesus is the only mediator between man and God.

3. Know that you have power and authority, according to Luke 10:19 and Genesis 1:26.

4. Put and keep on the entire armor of God (Ephesians 6:10–17).

A new level will require prayer as your first response, not your last resort. Don't get anxious but put on the entire armor of God and give thanks while he takes you higher.

Today's Reflection
Often the next level, or a new door, will require changing your environment and association, which may bring discomfort in the beginning. Continue to give God high praise and adoration; abide in him and give thanks in all circumstances. Have a strong belief in yourself to quiet all the outside noises.

Day Twenty-Eight
The Second Coming

Scripture: Matthew 24:1–51

Do not ignore the signs.

The disciples asked Jesus two questions regarding the second coming.

- When shall it be?

- What will the signs be?

Read the entire chapter of Matthew 24. As you read, you'll realize that you've already observed many of these signs.

Many have already been deceived; there are wars and rumours of wars, pandemics and pestilences, and betrayals; people are hated for Jesus's sake; nations are rising up against nations; many false prophets are rising by the day; and even the elect and chosen ones are being deceived.

The *meat* of it, according to Jesus, is that the society at the time of his second coming will be the same as in the days of Noah (see Matthew 24:37–39).

There is an assurance that if you endure to the end, you shall be saved (see Matthew 24:13).

Today's Reflection
We live in a time of multiple daily distractions, most of which reroute and detour our time. We must discern the time, as the days are evil (Ephesians 5:16), and see beyond what we can see and hear in the natural (Isaiah 11:3).

Abide in God, and he in you.

Stay ready!

Day Twenty-Nine

Victory in Jesus

Scripture: Matthew 28:1–10

We serve the risen Christ, the victorious one. Death couldn't hold him down. He reigns forever, and of his kingdom there is no end, from everlasting to everlasting.

When the victorious one lives in you, you can obtain victory in every area of your life, be it finances, health, career, and family. Many forces work against family and marriages, such as the evil magnets of strange activities that are planted behind the scenes. Let God be the glue in your home, place of worship, relationships, marriage, business, and school by attaining victory through Jesus.

Today's Reflection
Know that he is able to take you from crucified to victorious.

Day 30

The Great Commission

Scripture: Matthew 28:16–20

The Great Commission is the final command of Christ to spread the Word by preaching and teaching all nations. The main objective is to be a witness or to witness to.

A. If you are already saved and born again, you reach the unsaved.

B. If you are unsaved, get saved and be born again.

With God you are either hot or cold, in or out. There is no middle ground. He said in Revelation 3:16 that he would spue you out if you are lukewarm.

God promised Matthew 28:20 that he will be with you, even to the end.

Share the Kingdom of God with love and meekness and start in your household.

Today's Reflection

As you spread the Word of God, remember that you're a witness. Let the light of Jesus shine through you in love and meekness, with confidence in God.

Don't get into conflicts, for you're a witness for God, not a lawyer or judge. God doesn't need anyone to fight for him; in fact, he's your defender. He will fight for you, and you shall be at peace (Exodus 14:14).

Printed in Canada